THE SWEET TASTE OF FREEDOM:
THE CHOCOLATE SEDER HAGGADAH

A DELICIOUSLY FUN AND PLAYFUL
PASSOVER EXPERIENCE FOR ALL AGES!

This Chocolate Seder Haggadah is a project of
The Nonprofit Imagineers, blending Jewish tradition with
pure imagination to create a Passover experience
that is both meaningful and delicious.

The Sweet Taste of Freedom:
The Chocolate Seder Haggadah

Published by:
Inspired Multimedia Press

First Edition: 2025
ISBN: 979-8-9927434-0-1

Special Thanks
This Haggadah was created with love, laughter, and an unreasonable amount of chocolate. Thank you to all who contributed ideas, recipes, and enthusiasm to bring this delicious tradition to life.

For permissions, inquiries, or bulk orders, contact:
ben@thenonprofitimagineers.com

COOKED UP BY
THE NONPROFIT IMAGINEERS

This Chocolate Seder Haggadah is a project from the creative minds at **The Nonprofit Imagineers**, where we blend innovation, tradition, and a touch of whimsy to help synagogues, schools, and Jewish organizations engage their communities in new and meaningful ways.

To explore more imaginative projects, workshops, and resources designed to strengthen nonprofit and Jewish life, visit **TheNonprofitImagineers.com**.

ALSO FROM THE NONPROFIT IMAGINEERS:

The Nonprofit Imagineers Book Series

Cards Against Conformity - The Game

The Ideas Folder

More than 150 worksheets and articles

HOW TO USE THIS HAGGADAH

This Haggadah is designed to bring joy, creativity, and a little extra sweetness to your Passover celebration. Whether you're leading a Seder for young children, students, or adults, this Haggadah provides fun discussions, interactive rituals, and plenty of chocolatey goodness for all ages.

FOR YOUNG CHILDREN

Make the Seder hands-on and playful! Encourage kids to taste, dip, and explore as they learn the Passover story in a delicious, memorable way. Use the kid-friendly discussion questions on page 40 to spark curiosity, let them hunt for the chocolate Afikoman, and sing along with the fun chocolate-themed songs!

FOR STUDENTS

Turn the Seder into a fun, engaging learning experience! Have students debate chocolate-related Passover dilemmas, discuss the balance of bitter and sweet in history and life, and explore how tradition and creativity can coexist. Use the teen discussion prompts on page 41 to inspire deeper thinking while still keeping things light and interactive.

FOR ADULTS

Even grown-ups deserve a sweet and meaningful Seder! Enjoy wine and chocolate pairings, share hilarious food-related Passover debates, and use the adult discussion questions to connect tradition with modern life.

No matter who you are or how you celebrate, this Chocolate Seder Haggadah invites you to taste the richness of freedom, enjoy the sweetness of community, and make this Passover one to remember!

PLANNING YOUR CHOCOLATE SEDER

To make your Chocolate Seder as sweet and seamless as possible, we recommend reading through the entire Haggadah in advance so you can gather and prepare all the delicious treats you'll need.

To make things easier, flip to page 44 for a full shopping list. If you are holding your seder before or after Passover feel free to substitute or add items to the seder that aren't kosher for Passover.

Don't forget to check pages 32-35 of this Haggadah for mouthwatering recipes, and pages 36-39 for joyful songs to make your Seder extra special!

TAKE YOUR SEDER TO THE NEXT LEVEL: FREE ADD-ONS AWAIT!

Why stop at just the basics when you can make your Chocolate Seder even more fun and engaging? Head over to **MyChocolateSeder.com** for a treasure trove of free extras!

THE SEDER PLATE (CHOCOLATE EDITION!)

The Seder plate usually holds symbolic foods, but tonight, we're giving it a cocoa-inspired makeover:

MAROR (BITTER CHOCOLATE)
A piece of dark chocolate to remind us of the bitterness of slavery.

CHAROSET (CHOCOLATE SPREAD/NUTELLA MIX)
A deliciously sweet representation of the mortar used by the Israelites.
If you think charoset couldn't get any better, wait until you try the chocolate version on page 33!

KARPAS (FRUIT OR GREEN CANDY)
A dipped item symbolizing spring and renewal.

ZEROA (CHOCOLATE-COVERED PRETZEL STICK, DRUMSTICK ICE CREAM, OR COOKIE ROD)
Representing the paschal offering.

BEITZAH (CHOCOLATE TRUFFLE OR EGG-SHAPED CHOCOLATE)
A symbol of rebirth and hope.

MATZAH (CHOCOLATE-COVERED MATZAH OR CHOCOLATE GRAHAM CRACKER)
Because nothing says "humble bread of affliction" like a little chocolate.

THE ORDER OF THE CHOCOLATE SEDER

1. KADESH – קַדֵּשׁ

We sanctify the Seder with a blessing over hot cocoa instead of wine!

2. URCHATZ – וּרְחַץ

Instead of washing with water, imagine dipping your hands into a chocolate fountain!

3. KARPAS – כַּרְפַּס

Dipping fruit into chocolate reminds us that even sweetness can have its struggles.

4. YACHATZ – יַחַץ

Breaking the middle piece of chocolate matzah for the Afikoman (the golden ticket of the Seder!).

5. MAGGID – מַגִּיד

We tell the story of escaping Egypt... and the tragic lack of chocolate along the way.

6. RACHTZAH – רַחְצָה

Time for another hand-washing.

7. MOTZI MATZAH – מוֹצִי מַצָּה

We bless and eat chocolate-covered matzah.

8. MAROR – מָרוֹר

Instead of bitter herbs, we taste dark chocolate to recall the bitterness of slavery.

9. KORECH – כּוֹרֵךְ

The Hillel sandwich, but this time it's charoset and dark chocolate together!

10. SHULCHAN ORECH – שׁוּלְחָן עוֹרֵךְ

The festive meal—featuring as much chocolate as possible!

11. TZAFUN – צָפוּן

Find the hidden chocolate Afikoman and claim your sweet prize.

12. BARECH – בָּרֵךְ

We thank all those who made tonight's chocolate-filled freedom possible!

13. HALLEL – הַלֵּל

Songs of praise and joy, best performed while nibbling on leftover chocolate.

14. NIRTZAH – נִרְצָה

We conclude with gratitude and say:
L'shanah haba'ah b'Yerushalayim… im yoter shokolad!
Next year in Jerusalem… with even more chocolate!

KADESH

Welcome to the Chocolate Seder! We officially begin with
Kadesh, the blessing over our first cup. But tonight, instead
of wine, we raise a steaming mug of hot cocoa (or chocolate
milk for the little ones, and maybe something with a kick for
the grown-ups). Because why should grape juice have all the
fun?

We say the traditional blessing:

Baruch Atah Adonai,	בָּרוּךְ אַתָּה ה'
Eloheinu Melech HaOlam,	אֱלֹהֵינוּ מֶלֶךְ הָעוֹלָם,
Borei P'ri HaGafen.	בּוֹרֵא פְּרִי הַגָּפֶן.

Blessed are You, Adonai our God, Ruler of the Universe,
who creates the fruit of the vine.

Wait...fruit of the vine? Cocoa beans grow on trees, right?
Close enough. L'Chaim! To life, to freedom, and to the
magical powers of chocolate!

URCHATZ

Now that we've blessed the evening, it's time to wash our hands—but since this is a Chocolate Seder, we're going to imagine dipping our hands into a flowing chocolate fountain instead of plain old water. But resist the urge—sticky hands and Haggadah pages are not a good mix.

This hand-washing reminds us that we are preparing for something special. Just as we clean our hands, we cleanse our minds, making space for the delicious (and meaningful) experience ahead.

There is no blessing for this step—just a moment to pause and appreciate the joy of anticipation.

KARPAS

Now it's time for dipping! Traditionally, we take something green—symbolizing spring and renewal—and dip it into saltwater, representing the tears of our ancestors. But since this is a Chocolate Seder, we're doing things a little differently.

Instead of parsley, grab a piece of green apple, kiwi, or a green gummy candy—something fresh and bright. Dip it into chocolate sauce to remind us that even life's most bitter moments can be coated with a little sweetness.

Before we dip, we say the blessing:

Baruch Atah Adonai,　　　　　　　　בָּרוּךְ אַתָּה ה'
Eloheinu Melech HaOlam,　　　　אֱלֹהֵינוּ מֶלֶךְ הָעוֹלָם,
Borei P'ri HaAdamah.　　　　　　בּוֹרֵא פְּרִי הָאֲדָמָה.

Blessed are You, Adonai our God, Ruler of the Universe, who creates the fruit of the earth.

Now dip, eat, and enjoy! And remember, sometimes life's challenges are just waiting for the right moment to be dunked into something sweet.

YACHATZ

Time to break the matzah—or in this case, the chocolate-covered matzah!

We take the middle piece and split it in two. The smaller half stays on the table, while the larger is hidden away as the Afikoman—the dessert we'll need to find later to finish the Seder. Think of it as the golden ticket of the Seder—hidden away until the lucky finder claims their chocolatey prize!

Just like this matzah, life isn't always whole. There are moments when things feel broken, incomplete, or hidden from us. But just as we will later find and enjoy the Afikoman, we trust that wholeness and sweetness can return.

MAGGID

Now comes the heart of the Seder—the story of our journey from bitterness to sweetness, from slavery to freedom. And what better way to tell a story than with chocolate?

Once upon a time, in a land far, far away (also known as Egypt), the Israelites were trapped in a life without choice, freedom... or dessert. Day after day, they worked under the scorching sun, dreaming of a better future. But one man, Moses, stood up and said, "Let my people go!" And so began an epic journey—one filled with obstacles, plagues, and a dramatic escape through the sea.

We tell this story every year because freedom isn't just something that happened in the past—it's something we strive for every day. And just like chocolate, freedom is best when shared.

THE FOUR QUESTIONS (MAH NISHTANAH)

Why is tonight different from all other nights? Well, for starters, there's way more chocolate.

Mah nishtanah ha-lailah hazeh mikol ha-leilot?

מַה נִּשְׁתַּנָּה הַלַּיְלָה הַזֶּה מִכָּל הַלֵּילוֹת?

Why is this night different from all other nights?

Just like the traditional *Mah Nishtanah*, we don't actually read four questions - we read a single question, and suggest four answers.

THE FOUR ANSWERS

On all other nights, we eat whatever we want. Tonight, we eat chocolate-covered matzah.

On all other nights, we eat vegetables. Tonight, we only eat foods that mix well with chocolate.

On all other nights, we don't dip our foods. Tonight, we double-dip in chocolate.

On all other nights, some eat and drink sitting, while others recline. Tonight, we all lean back and savor every bite.

HA LACHMA ANYA – THIS IS THE BREAD OF AFFLICTION

We lift up the chocolate-covered matzah and say:

Ha lachma anya di achalu	הָא לַחְמָא עַנְיָא דִּי אֲכָלוּ
avahatana b'ara d'mitzrayim.	אַבְהָתָנָא בְּאַרְעָא דְמִצְרָיִם.
Kol dichfin yeitei v'yeichol,	כָּל דִּכְפִין יֵיתֵי וְיֵיכוֹל,
kol ditzrich yeitei v'yifsach.	כָּל דִּצְרִיךְ יֵיתֵי וְיִפְסַח.

This is the bread of affliction that our ancestors ate in the land of Egypt (well, except for the chocolate coating). Let all who are hungry come and eat. Let all who are in need join our Passover meal.

Matzah is called the "bread of affliction," but tonight it's the "chocolate-covered bread of affliction." If only the Israelites had access the array of cocoa products we have today! Still, we remember that not everyone is free, and it is our duty to help those in need.

THE TEN PLAGUES

Check out page 30 for a fun alternative ritual!
When Pharaoh refused to let the Israelites go, Egypt was hit with ten plagues. Tonight, we remember them... but in chocolate form.

As we recite the plagues, we dip our fingers into chocolate milk, removing a drop from our glass, remembering the suffering of the Egyptians and the cost of freedom.

BLOOD
Chocolate syrup in the Nile!

FROGS
Chocolate frogs (hello, Harry Potter fans).

LICE
Chocolate sprinkles everywhere!

WILD ANIMALS
Chocolate animal crackers running amok.

CATTLE DISEASE
No more chocolate milk!

BOILS
Pop Rocks or chocolate-covered raisins bursting... ewww!

HAIL
White chocolate chips raining down!

LOCUSTS
Chocolate-covered almonds (because they crunch like locusts).

DARKNESS
Chocolate blackout cake.

DEATH OF THE FIRSTBORN
A moment of pause: even in joy, we remember real struggles.

DAYENU

At our Seder, we sing *Dayenu*, a song of gratitude. Traditionally, *Dayenu* reminds us of the many blessings we have received—each one alone would have been enough. Tonight, we sing *Dayenu* with a sweet twist, celebrating the gift of chocolate and all its delicious forms!

Ilu natan natan lanu	אִלוּ נָתַן נָתַן לָנוּ
Natan lanu et ha-pulei kakao,	נָתַן לָנוּ אֶת הַפּוּלֵי קָקוֹאָה,
Natan lanu et ha-pulei kakao,	נָתַן לָנוּ אֶת הַפּוּלֵי קָקוֹאָה,
Dayenu!	דַּיֵּנוּ!

Ilu natan natan lanu	אִלוּ נָתַן נָתַן לָנוּ
Natan lanu et ha-shokolad ha-marir,	נָתַן לָנוּ אֶת הַשּׁוֹקוֹלָד הַמָּרִיר,
Natan lanu et ha-shokolad ha-marir,	נָתַן לָנוּ אֶת הַשּׁוֹקוֹלָד הַמָּרִיר,
Dayenu!	דַּיֵּנוּ!

Ilu natan natan lanu	אִלוּ נָתַן נָתַן לָנוּ
Natan lanu et ha-shokolad ha-chalavi,	נָתַן לָנוּ אֶת הַשּׁוֹקוֹלָד הַחֲלָבִי,
Natan lanu et ha-shokolad ha-chalavi,	נָתַן לָנוּ אֶת הַשּׁוֹקוֹלָד הַחֲלָבִי,
Dayenu!	דַּיֵּנוּ!

Ilu natan natan lanu	אִלוּ נָתַן נָתַן לָנוּ
Natan lanu et ha-shokolad ha-memule,	נָתַן לָנוּ אֶת הַשּׁוֹקוֹלָד הַמְמוּלָּא
Natan lanu et ha-shokolad ha-memule,	נָתַן לָנוּ אֶת הַשּׁוֹקוֹלָד הַמְמוּלָּא
Dayenu!	דַּיֵּנוּ!

If God had given us cocoa beans, it would have been enough!
If God had given us dark chocolate, it would have been enough!
If God had given us milk chocolate, it would have been enough!
If God had given us filled chocolate, it would have been enough!

But we have so much more than just these forms of chocolate!
Dayenu teaches us that we should be grateful for each step, not just the final result. Tonight, we give thanks for every step of chocolate's journey—from bean to bar to our taste buds!

THE FOUR CHILDREN... OR CHOCOLATE PERSONALITIES

In every generation, we tell the story of Passover in different ways, because everyone learns and understands in their own style. Traditionally, the Haggadah speaks of four children—each with a different attitude toward the Seder. But tonight, let's imagine chocolate as if it had a personality, each type with its own unique take on the Passover experience.

THE WISE CHILD
Milk Chocolate: Smooth and Thoughtful

The wise child asks:
"What are the deeper meanings behind the customs of the Seder?"

This child wants to understand everything—the history, the traditions, the symbolism, and the significance of every delicious bite. They savor their chocolate just like they savor knowledge, taking their time to appreciate every rich layer.

How do we respond?
We explain everything in detail, from why we dip twice to the origins of the Chocolate Seder itself. Because when someone is eager to learn, we share everything we can!

THE WICKED CHILD
Dark Chocolate: Bold and Slightly Bitter

The wicked child asks:
"What does this Seder mean to you?" (a.k.a., "Why should I care?")

This child stands slightly apart, questioning the whole experience. They might roll their eyes at the traditions or say, "This is just a lot of work for a little matzah and some chocolate."

How do we respond?
We remind them that freedom isn't just about personal choice—it's about community. Just like chocolate is best when shared, so too is our history. The Seder is for all of us, whether we feel like participants or observers.

THE SIMPLE CHILD
White Chocolate: Sweet and Curious

The simple child asks:
"What is this all about?"

This child doesn't overcomplicate things. They just want to know why we're here and why we're eating all this chocolate! They take in the Seder with wide-eyed wonder, eager to enjoy the sweetness of the moment.

How do we respond?
We keep it simple: "We were slaves, and now we are free. And we celebrate that freedom together." Sometimes, the simplest answers are the sweetest.

THE CHILD WHO DOES NOT KNOW HOW TO ASK
A Chocolate Surprise: Full of Potential!

This child doesn't even know what to ask, either because they're too young, too shy, or just overwhelmed by all the chocolatey goodness.

How do we respond?

We bring them in with warmth and sweetness, just like offering a bite of a new chocolate bar and saying, "Here, try this." We tell the story in a way that includes them, making it engaging, playful, and welcoming. Because the Seder isn't just about knowing what to ask—it's about being part of the experience.

THE SECOND CUP OF CHOCOLATE (OR WINE!)

We lift our second cup of chocolate milk (or cocoa, or chocolate liqueur) and drink to the sweetness of freedom. Just like chocolate, freedom is something to be savored, cherished, and shared. No need for a blessing this time because, let's be honest, it was a bit of a stretch to call cocoa beans "fruit of the vine" the first time!

RACHTZAH

We've made it halfway through the Seder, and it's time to wash our hands again—but this time, with a blessing! Think of it as a chocolate intermission before we dive deeper into the sweetness of the evening.

As you dip your hands in water, imagine dipping your hands into warm, flowing chocolate. This washing is about preparing ourselves for what comes next, cleansing not just our hands but our hearts as we move forward in the Seder.

We say the blessing:

Baruch Atah Adonai,	בָּרוּךְ אַתָּה ה'
Eloheinu Melech HaOlam,	אֱלֹהֵינוּ מֶלֶךְ הָעוֹלָם,
Asher kid'shanu b'mitzvotav	אֲשֶׁר קִדְּשָׁנוּ בְּמִצְוֹתָיו
v'tzivanu al netilat yadayim.	וְצִוָּנוּ עַל נְטִילַת יָדָיִם.

Blessed are You, Adonai our God, Ruler of the Universe, who sanctifies us with mitzvot and commands us to wash our hands.

Now, with clean hands and ready hearts, we continue the journey!

MOTZI MATZAH

It's finally time to eat the matzah! But since this is a Chocolate Seder, we're not just eating any matzah—we're indulging in chocolate-covered matzah because freedom should taste amazing.

We begin with the traditional blessing over bread:

Baruch Atah Adonai,
Eloheinu Melech HaOlam,
ha-motzi lechem min ha-aretz.

בָּרוּךְ אַתָּה ה'
אֱלֹהֵינוּ מֶלֶךְ הָעוֹלָם,
הַמּוֹצִיא לֶחֶם מִן הָאָרֶץ.

Blessed are You, Adonai our God, Ruler of the Universe, who brings forth bread from the earth.

Since matzah isn't exactly fluffy bread, we also say a special blessing:

Baruch Atah Adonai,
Eloheinu Melech HaOlam,
asher kid'shanu b'mitzvotav
v'tzivanu al achilat matzah.

בָּרוּךְ אַתָּה ה'
אֱלֹהֵינוּ מֶלֶךְ הָעוֹלָם,
אֲשֶׁר קִדְּשָׁנוּ בְּמִצְוֹתָיו
וְצִוָּנוּ עַל אֲכִילַת מַצָּה.

Blessed are You, Adonai our God, Ruler of the Universe, who sanctifies us with mitzvot and commands us to eat matzah.

Now, take a bite! Crunchy, sweet, and a little messy—just like the journey to freedom.

MAROR

Sweetness is wonderful, but life isn't always dipped in chocolate. Maror, the bitter herb, reminds us of the bitterness of slavery and the hardships of the past. But don't worry—we're still keeping things delicious!

Tonight, instead of traditional horseradish, we take a bite of bitter dark chocolate—the really bitter stuff—at least 85% cacao. It's a reminder that freedom wasn't easy and that even in a world full of sweetness, we must never forget the struggles that came before.

Before eating, we say the blessing:

Baruch Atah Adonai,	בָּרוּךְ אַתָּה ה'
Eloheinu Melech HaOlam,	אֱלֹהֵינוּ מֶלֶךְ הָעוֹלָם,
asher kid'shanu b'mitzvotav	אֲשֶׁר קִדְּשָׁנוּ בְּמִצְוֹתָיו
v'tzivanu al achilat maror.	וְצִוָּנוּ עַל אֲכִילַת מָרוֹר.

Blessed are You, Adonai our God, Ruler of the Universe, who sanctifies us with mitzvot and commands us to eat maror.

Now, take a bite! Bitter, isn't it? A stark contrast to the sweetness of our chocolate matzah. It's a reminder that appreciating the sweet moments in life often comes from understanding the bitter ones.

KORECH

It's time for the ultimate Seder sandwich! Hillel, the famous rabbi, came up with this brilliant idea: combine the bitterness of maror, the plainness of matzah, and a touch of sweet from charoset, to create a balanced bite. Since this is a Chocolate Seder, we're going to upgrade Hillel's idea—sweet and bitter together in one delicious bite!

Tonight, we make our Chocolate Hillel Sandwich by layering:

A piece of chocolate-covered matzah
(representing freedom)

A chunk of dark chocolate
(representing bitterness)

A spread of chocolate charoset
(representing the hard work of the Israelites)

Now, take a bite! Bittersweet, crunchy, messy, and totally delicious—just like life.

SHULCHAN ORECH

Finally! It's time for the festive meal—a moment of joy, celebration, and, of course, chocolate!

Since every Seder meal is different, we encourage you to make this one as chocolate-filled as possible. If you're on chocolate overload, don't worry—feel free to take a break with something salty before diving back in!

As we enjoy this meal together, we reflect on what it means to sit at a table filled with abundance, laughter, and the people we love.

TALK AMONGST YOURSELVES: WE'LL GIVE YOU SOME TOPICS.

Check pages 40-42 for fun and engaging Chocolate Seder discussion questions for all ages to enjoy while savoring your meal.

TZAFUN

The moment we've all been waiting for… the Great Chocolate Afikoman Hunt!

Earlier in the Seder, we broke a piece of chocolate-covered matzah and hid it away. Now, it's time to find the Afikoman, because no Seder (or Chocolate Seder) can end without it!

Whoever finds the Afikoman gets a special chocolatey prize—maybe an extra-large chocolate bar, a golden-wrapped truffle, or just the honor of being the Chocolate Champion of the Seder.

Once it's found, we take a bite together, because in the end, we all share in the sweetness of freedom.

The final taste of matzah, the final taste of chocolate, and the final reminder that freedom is something to be celebrated— every day, in every way.

BARECH

We've eaten, we've laughed, we've indulged in so much chocolate—now it's time to give thanks. The word *Barech* means "blessing," and this is our moment to pause, reflect, and express gratitude for the food we've enjoyed and the freedom we celebrate.

We recite a short version of *Birkat Hamazon*, the blessing after meals:

Baruch Atah Adonai,	בָּרוּךְ אַתָּה ה'
Eloheinu Melech HaOlam,	אֱלֹהֵינוּ מֶלֶךְ הָעוֹלָם,
hazan et ha'olam kulo b'tuvo,	הַזָּן אֶת הָעוֹלָם כֻּלּוֹ בְּטוּבוֹ,
b'chein, b'chesed uv'rachamim.	בְּחֵן, בְּחֶסֶד וּבְרַחֲמִים.

Blessed are You, Adonai our God, Ruler of the Universe, who nourishes the entire world with goodness, grace, kindness, and compassion.

Just like chocolate is a gift, so too is freedom. Tonight, we give thanks not just for food, but for the sweetness of life, for being together, and for the ability to celebrate in joy.

THE THIRD CUP OF CHOCOLATE (OR WINE!)

At this point, we raise our mugs (or glasses) once more and drink our third cup of hot cocoa, chocolate milk, or wine. Gratitude is best when sipped slowly.

HALLEL

Now that our stomachs are full (mostly of chocolate), it's time to sing, celebrate, and give thanks! *Hallel* means "praise," and tonight, we lift our voices in joyful gratitude for freedom, for community, and—of course—for the miracle of chocolate.

We start with this blessing:

Baruch Atah Adonai,	בָּרוּךְ אַתָּה ה'
Eloheinu Melech HaOlam,	אֱלֹהֵינוּ מֶלֶךְ הָעוֹלָם,
asher natan lanu simcha	אֲשֶׁר נָתַן לָנוּ שִׂמְחָה
v'hodayah, l'hallel et Hashem	וְהוֹדָיָה, לְהַלֵּל אֶת הַשֵׁם
b'shir u'v'zimrah.	בְּשִׁיר וּבְזִמְרָה.

Blessed are You, Adonai our God, Ruler of the Universe, who has given us joy and gratitude, to praise Your name in song and melody.

Traditionally, we sing from Psalms, but in the spirit of the Chocolate Seder, feel free to get creative. Make up your own songs, or turn to pages 36-39 for a few fun ones.

THE FOURTH CUP – THE SWEETEST SIP

We raise our final cup of hot cocoa, chocolate milk, or wine, and take a grateful sip, savoring the sweetness of freedom and tradition.

NIRTZAH

We've dipped, we've sung, we've eaten our weight in chocolate, and now we've reached the final step of the Seder—*Nirtzah*, the conclusion.

Tonight, we've relived the journey from slavery to freedom, and we've done it in the sweetest way possible. But the real message of Passover isn't just about what happened in the past—it's about what comes next. How do we bring more freedom, kindness, and maybe even a little more chocolate into the world?

As we close our Seder, we say together:

L'shanah haba'ah b'Yerushalayim!　　　　!לְשָׁנָה הַבָּאָה בִּירוּשָׁלָיִם

Next year in Jerusalem!

...And for this special Chocolate Seder:

L'shanah haba'ah b'Yerushalayim,　　　　,לְשָׁנָה הַבָּאָה בִּירוּשָׁלַיִם
im yoter shokolad!　　　　　　　　　!עִם יוֹתֵר שׁוֹקוֹלָד

Next year in Jerusalem...
with even more chocolate!

THE 10 PLAGUES ALTERNATIVE CANDY RITUAL

Instead of dipping our fingers in chocolate milk and removing a drop for each plague, we will remove a piece of candy from a special Plagues Bowl and place it into a to-go container. This reminds us that while we celebrate our freedom, we also carry the memory of hardship with us—but in this case, we take it home in a sweet, symbolic way!

Each bowl contains a different type of candy or snack that represents a plague, adding an interactive and delicious twist to the Seder.

Blood – Red Gummy Worms or Red Licorice
The Nile turned to blood, undrinkable and terrifying. Take a red gummy worm or licorice to symbolize the river running red.

Frogs – Chocolate Frogs or Gummy Frogs
Frogs covered the land—jumping into homes, beds, and food! Take a chocolate or gummy frog as a reminder of their sticky invasion.

Lice – Chocolate Sprinkles or Nerds Candy
Tiny, itchy lice tormented the Egyptians. Take a pinch of chocolate sprinkles or Nerds to symbolize the tiny pests that got everywhere!

Wild Beasts – Animal Crackers or Gummy Bears
The land was filled with roaring, dangerous creatures. Take an animal cracker or gummy bear to represent the wild beasts.

Cattle Disease – Milky Way or Cow Tales Candy
The Egyptian livestock fell ill. Take a Milky Way bar or Cow Tales candy to represent the cattle affected by disease.

Boils – Pop Rocks or Chocolate Raisins

Painful boils covered everyone's skin. Take Pop Rocks (to symbolize the burning sensation) or chocolate-covered raisins (for the bumps on the skin).

Hail – Mini Marshmallows or White Chocolate Chips

Hail rained down from the sky, destroying crops and homes. Take a mini marshmallow or white chocolate chip to represent the icy destruction.

Locusts – Chocolate-Covered Almonds or Crickets – if you dare!

Locusts devoured all the crops. Take a chocolate-covered almond (representing crunchy locusts) or, for the bold, a chocolate-covered cricket!

Darkness – Dark Chocolate Pieces or Black Licorice

A thick, terrifying darkness covered the land. Take a piece of dark chocolate or black licorice to symbolize the absence of light.

Death of the Firstborn – Sour Patch Kids

The final plague struck the firstborn in every household. Take a Sour Patch Kid - The sourness reminds us of the pain of loss, while the sweetness reflects the hope and redemption that followed.

The Sweet Takeaway

At the end of the Seder, everyone will have a small to-go box or bag filled with these "plagues" in candy form. This symbolizes that we carry the memory of hardship with us, even as we celebrate freedom. But in this Chocolate Seder, we also recognize that from struggle comes sweetness—and that even the hardest moments can be transformed into something we share together.

RECIPES

PASSOVER CHOCOLATE BROWNIES

Fudgy, chewy, and totally flourless!

Ingredients:
½ cup unsalted butter or coconut oil
1 cup semisweet chocolate chips (Passover-friendly)
¾ cup sugar
2 eggs
1 tsp vanilla extract
¼ cup unsweetened cocoa powder
¼ cup almond flour or ground walnuts
¼ tsp salt

Directions:
Preheat oven to 350°F (175°C) and grease an 8x8-inch baking dish.
Melt the butter and chocolate chips together in a microwave-safe bowl (stir every 30 seconds until smooth).
Stir in sugar, then beat in eggs and vanilla until smooth.
Add cocoa powder, almond flour, and salt. Mix until just combined.
Pour into the baking dish and bake for 20-25 minutes, until the center is just set.
Cool completely before cutting (if you can wait that long!).

Optional: Top with melted chocolate and a sprinkle of sea salt for extra indulgence!

CHOCOLATE CHAROSET

A rich, chocolatey take on the classic Passover charoset!

Ingredients:
2 apples, finely chopped (Granny Smith for tartness or Honeycrisp for sweetness)
½ cup finely chopped walnuts or almonds
¼ cup chocolate chips (Passover-friendly)
2 tbsp unsweetened cocoa powder
2 tbsp honey or maple syrup
1 tsp cinnamon
¼ tsp salt
sweet red wine or grape juice

Directions:
In a bowl, mix the apples, nuts, cinnamon, and salt.
Melt the chocolate chips in the microwave (30-second bursts, stirring in between).
Stir the melted chocolate, cocoa powder, and honey into the apple mixture.
Slowly add the wine or grape juice and mix until everything is well coated.
Let sit for at least 30 minutes to allow the flavors to meld.
Serve with chocolate-covered matzah or by the spoonful!

Optional: Add a dash of orange zest for an extra kick!

CRAVING MORE? FIND EXTRA RECIPES ONLINE!
Want more ways to indulge? Find additional Chocolate Seder recipes at MyChocolateSeder.com!

PASSOVER S'MORES BITES

No campfire needed—just crunchy, gooey, chocolatey perfection!

Ingredients:
1 cup chocolate chips (Passover-friendly)
½ cup mini marshmallows
4 sheets of matzah, broken into squares
¼ cup almond butter (optional, for extra richness)

Directions:
Preheat oven to 350°F (175°C).
Place matzah squares on a baking sheet.
Spread almond butter on half of them (optional).
Sprinkle chocolate chips and mini marshmallows on top.
Bake for 5-7 minutes, just until the chocolate melts and marshmallows get golden.
Sandwich with another matzah square and enjoy!

Optional: Use white chocolate for a twist on the classic!

CHOCOLATE MATZAH BARK

The easiest and most addictive Passover treat!

Ingredients:
3 Matzos
1 cup unsalted butter
1 cup packed brown sugar
12 oz semisweet chocolate chips
¼ cup chopped nuts, dried fruit, or coconut flakes (optional)

Directions:
Line a baking sheet with parchment paper. Place matzah sheets on top.
Melt butter and brown sugar, stirring occasionally, for 5 minutes. Pour over matzah and spread evenly.
Bake for 5 minutes in 400 degree oven.
Sprinkle chocolate chips and allow to melt for 2 minutes.
Spread melted chocolate evenly and sprinkle with sea salt and optional toppings (nuts, coconut, or dried fruit).
Chill in the fridge for at least 1 hour, then break into pieces.

CHOCOLATE SEDER MUSIC

"HALLELUJAH (FOR CHOCOLATE)"
(TO THE TUNE OF "HALLELUJAH" BY LEONARD COHEN)

We raise our mugs, we sing with joy,
This night is sweet for each girl and boy,
And every bite reminds us we are free, yeah!

With matzah crisp and chocolate fine,
This Seder meal is so divine,
And so we say a joyful Hallelujah!

(Chorus)
Hallelujah, Hallelujah,
Hallelujah, for chocolate too-oo-oo-yah!

"OH CHOCOLATE NIGHT"
(TO THE TUNE OF "O HOLY NIGHT")

Oh chocolate night, the stars are brightly shining,
This is the night, our Seder fills with cheer!
Long was our past, but now we taste redemption,
With cocoa joy, we celebrate this year!

Sweet is the taste of matzah dipped in caramel,
Dark chocolate's bold, yet freedom's sweeter still!
Raise up your cup! This Seder is delightful,
Eat and rejoice, eat and rejoice—
For chocolate is divine!

"DON'T STOP THE SEDER"
(TO THE TUNE OF "DON'T STOP BELIEVIN'" BY JOURNEY)

Just a kid in Egypt town,
Trapped and working, feeling down,
Then Moses came and said it's time to go!

Now we're free and drinking shakes,
Matzah's here and there's no cake,
But chocolate makes it all taste great, we know!

(Chorus)
Don't stop the Seder!
Pass the brownies all around!
Sweet freedom's here now!
With chocolate, joy abounds!

"CUPS OF CHOCOLATE"
(TO THE TUNE OF "MY FAVORITE THINGS" FROM THE SOUND OF MUSIC)

Cups full of cocoa and matzah with truffle,
Drizzling fudge makes my knees start to buckle!
Charoset with chocolate, oh what joy it brings,
These are a few of my favorite things!

When the milk spills,
When the sauce burns,
When I'm feeling sad,
I simply remember my favorite treats—
And then I don't feel so bad!

"PASS THE CHOCOLATE 'ROUND"
(TO THE TUNE OF "SHAKE IT OFF" BY TAYLOR SWIFT)

'Cause the Seder's gonna
start, start, start, start, start,

And the cocoa's gonna
flow, flow, flow, flow, flow,

So we'll pass the chocolate
'round, 'round, 'round, 'round, 'round,

Drink it down, drink it down!

Yeah, the matzah's gonna
 crunch, crunch, crunch, crunch, crunch,

And the brownies gonna
munch, munch, munch, munch, munch,

So we'll pass the chocolate
'round, 'round, 'round, 'round, 'round,

And sing this Hallel loud!

KEEP THE CHOCOLATEY TUNES FLOWING!
There's always room for more music!
Discover extra Passover songs at
MyChocolateSeder.com!

"MOSES ATE SOME CHOCOLATE"
(TO THE TUNE OF "SHE'LL BE COMING 'ROUND THE MOUNTAIN")

Moses ate some chocolate in the desert, yes he did!
(Yes he did!)

Moses ate some chocolate in the desert, yes he did!
(Yes he did!)

He had matzah, he had fudge,

Though the journey was a trudge,

Moses ate some chocolate in the desert, yes he did!

When we left old Pharaoh's land, we grabbed some snacks!
(We grabbed some snacks!)

When we left old Pharaoh's land, we grabbed some snacks!
(We grabbed some snacks!)

We had matzah, we had spread,

A chocolate Seder in our heads,

When we left old Pharaoh's land, we grabbed some snacks!

TOPICS FOR CONVERSATION

YOUNG CHILDREN (ELEMENTARY SCHOOL AGED)

If you could create a new chocolate Jewish holiday, what would it be called and how would we celebrate it?

How does chocolate remind us of the story of Passover?

If Pharaoh had to give Moses a giant chocolate apology gift, what kind of chocolate treat should he send?

What's the best chocolate and fruit combination? Chocolate-covered strawberries, bananas, or apples?

If the Ten Plagues were replaced with chocolate disasters, what would be the funniest ones? (e.g., chocolate rain, a flood of sprinkles)

If Moses and Pharaoh each had a favorite kind of chocolate, what do you think it would be and why?

Which would be harder: giving up chocolate for a whole year or being stuck eating only chocolate for a whole year?

If you could invite any cartoon character to the Chocolate Seder, who would it be and why?

What's the weirdest thing you think might taste good covered in chocolate?

If you could invent a brand new type of chocolate, what would it be called, and what flavor would it have?

TEENS

Is white chocolate actually chocolate, or is it an impostor? Debate!

If you were on a deserted island and could only bring one kind of chocolate, which would you choose and why?

Would you rather eat chocolate-covered matzah for a week straight or not eat chocolate for a year?

If you could make a new version of the Four Questions, but all about chocolate, what would one of them be?

What's worse: burnt chocolate, grainy chocolate, or accidentally dropping your chocolate in water?

In your real seder, if you could swap one Passover tradition for a chocolate-related tradition, what would you change and why?

If the Israelites had chocolate in the desert, how would that have changed the story?

Which would be harder to give up for a whole month: chocolate or social media?

Milk chocolate, dark chocolate, and white chocolate are all different, but they're still chocolate. What does this teach us about diversity in Jewish communities?

What kind of chocolate best represents Moses, Pharaoh, and Miriam, and why?

ADULTS

What's the greatest chocolate invention of all time—and what is the most overrated chocolate trend?

Milk chocolate vs. dark chocolate—which is superior, and why?

If you had to pair wine with chocolate, what's the best combination?

If Passover desserts could include flour, would we even still bother with flourless chocolate cake?

If you could create a Jewish holiday entirely based on chocolate, what traditions would it have?

What other verses would you add to the Chocolate Seder *Dayenu*?

If you had to survive a real Passover Seder where every food was chocolate-based, which dish would be the biggest challenge?

If Moses had had chocolate to bribe Pharaoh, would the Exodus have happened faster?

If you could host a celebrity Chocolate Seder, who would you invite and why?

What's the most creative way to use chocolate in a Seder dish that hasn't been done before?

CHOCOLATE SEDER SHOPPING LIST

SEDER PLATE INGREDIENTS

Dark chocolate bar or bittersweet chocolate
Chocolate Charoset, Chocolate spread, Nutella
Green fruit (kiwi, green apple, or green gummy candy)
Drumbstick ice cream or chocolate-covered wafer sticks
Chocolate truffle or egg-shaped chocolate
Chocolate-covered matzah or graham crackers

FOUR CUPS OF CHOCOLATE

Chocolate milk, hot cocoa, or chocolate liqueur
Whipped cream, cinnamon, or marshmallows (optional, for topping your cocoa)

10 PLAGUES CANDY
(FOR THE PLAGUE RITUAL ON PAGE 30)

Red licorice or gummy worms (Blood)
Chocolate frogs or gummy frogs (Frogs)
Chocolate sprinkles or Nerds candy (Lice)
Animal crackers or gummy bears (Wild Beasts)
Milky Way bars or Cow Tales candy (Cattle Disease)
Pop Rocks or chocolate-covered raisins (Boils)
Mini marshmallows or white chocolate chips (Hail)
Chocolate-covered almonds or chocolate crickets (if you're brave!) (Locusts)
Dark chocolate squares or black licorice (Darkness)
Sour Patch Kids (Death of the Firstborn)
To-go boxes or bags

EXTRAS FOR FUN & AMBIANCE

Decorations in chocolatey colors (brown, gold, and cream)
Chocolate-scented candles (if you want to go all-in on the theme!)
Small prize for the Afikoman winner (extra chocolate, of course!)

A NOTE ABOUT CHOCOLATE AND MODERN-DAY SLAVERY

As we celebrate our freedom with sweet treats and laughter, it's important to remember that slavery still exists in our world today. Many of the cocoa beans used to make chocolate are grown and harvested by children and adults who are forced to work in unsafe, unfair conditions—especially in parts of West Africa. This reality stands in painful contrast to the joy we experience tonight.

That's why it's meaningful to choose fair trade chocolate whenever possible—chocolate that comes from farms where workers are treated with dignity and paid fairly. By making thoughtful choices, we honor the true spirit of Passover: not just remembering our own journey to freedom, but working to ensure freedom for others too.

EVERYTHING YOU NEED FOR A SWEET SEDER, ALL IN ONE PLACE!

From frog and wild beast candy molds to chocolate-scented candles, we've got [almost] everything you need to make your Chocolate Seder unforgettable! Visit MyChocolateSeder.com to stock up today.

PHOTO CREDITS

YOU FOUND THE SECRET BONUS PAGE!

Congratulations! You've reached the final, completely unnecessary, yet totally delightful page of this Chocolate Seder Haggadah. I can't believe you actually read past the photo credits!

You now have two choices:

1. Take a moment to reflect on the meaning of Passover, the richness of freedom, and the ongoing debate: is chocolate-covered matzah an upgrade or a betrayal of tradition?

2. Watch everyone at the table make a fool of themselves when they scratch and sniff below, and then say they smell chocolate... HINT: it doesn't smell like anything.

Either way, remember: Next year in Jerusalem... with even more chocolate!